LOVE
LIFE
TO
DEATH

Susan Crane

LOVE LIFE TO DEATH

First paperback edition 2023

Book design by Susan Crane

ISBN 979-8-9893373-1-6

TABLE OF CONTENTS

Finding Susan	1
What Can't be Undone	2
I Want to Live	3
Regrets	4
Forever Love	5
Enter Player 2	7
Maybe One Day	8
Stay	9
True Love	10
Last Pear	11
Pink Flamingo	11
My Way	12
Her Name	13
Sometimes	15
The Veil	16
Was it a Dream	17
Now and Forever	19
Wishing	20
Dream	21
?	22
Dirt	22
Tired	23
The Rainbow	24
Ramble	25
Death	26
Yo, Bro	27
26 Copycat Trail	28
A Day in the Life of a Slug	29
Mini Golf Day	30
Why I Like Being a Cat	30

TABLE OF CONTENTS

Hands of You and I	31
The Man in the Red Coat	32
Alone	33
Issues	34
Social Media Stalking	35
Down by the River	36
Turn and Run Cue	37
Eulogy	38
Searching	39
Girl	40
Boat	41
Just Be You	42
Tommy	43
The Bridge	45
Hit with Reality	47
They	49
Bury the Past	50
Music from Within	51
These Thoughts	53
Running Scared	55
Anxious Memory	57
Fate	58
Fighting History	59
I Will Shelter You	61
It's Been A Long Day	63
No Need	64
All Alone	65
Abduction	66
Living on a Lyric	67
Take and Break	68

TABLE OF CONTENTS

Black Sheep	69
When	70
Disappointment	71
Invasion	73
Girlhawk	74
Violence is Not Love	75
Moving Forward	76
Sad Songs	77
Can't Undo	78
The Letter	79
Life	80
Fear	81
Secret	82
I Survived You	83
Mourning	84
Skeletons in Your Closet	85
Live	86
The War in My Head	87
Raining Since November	88
Dear Susan	91
A Letter to Myself	92

PREFACE

Welcome to the thoughts that are inside my head at
any given moment.

From a young age I experienced trauma and abuse
from all avenues of life. Art in some form was always
a way for me to release emotions even if they were not
always understood. This book, this work of art, has in
some ways been a life saver. It has opened my eyes to
move past the hurt, anger, lies and fears. It has helped
me be in tune with love, happiness, laughter and even
cope with loss.

People say the past makes you who you are, but I am
learning that is not true. I decide who I am and who I
want to be. I am learning that life is not a destination
and you do not have to stay within the confines of
pain. If someone or something is hurting you, there is
an option to move on and heal.

This started out as just some poems I wanted to share
with the world and has become an adventure I did not
know I needed.

If you or someone you know are dealing with domestic violence, thoughts of hurting yourself or others or any type of abuse there is help waiting.

NATIONAL DOMESTIC VIOLENCE HOTLINE

Call: 800-799-7233

Text: START to 88788

SUICIDE AND CRISIS LIFELINE

Call: 988

Text: 988

ACKNOWLEDGMENTS

PHILIP CRANE:

To my husband, my knight in rusted armor, everyday with you is an adventure. You continuously show me what unconditional love means and encourage me to be myself. This book was my dream that you helped make come true. From the times you listened to every word I wrote, to the times that you inspired some words to be written. You have given me space and time to work through some incredibly rough memories and emotions. You have stood by me during the dark times and danced with me in the bright times. I am truly blessed by God with your love, encouragement, determination and belief in my art. I love you!

DENISE C. POWELL LCSW, CEAP:

You are an amazing human that I am incredibly grateful to have with me on this journey. Your company, wisdom, inspiration, support and guidance have brought me great comfort. Publishing a book of poetry is a dream I had put on a shelf, never to be taken down. That all changed the day you encouraged me to once again put my thoughts on paper. Thank you from the bottom of my heart for believing in me and pushing me to believe in myself. Without you I would still be lost in the dark and wondering if I would ever again see the light. Your guidance has made it possible to begin to break free from the hurt that I carried from my past and inspired the growth that has taken place during this process.

ACKNOWLEDGMENTS

Tanner Rutledge:

My birthday twin (haha), you are an inspiration. Thank you for reigniting a fire for storytelling that I thought had long been extinguished. Your inspiration, motivation and just pure love for writing has meant a great deal to me from the start of this journey.

Brandon Eason:

You are awesome. Thank you for all of the advice and time you have provided in terms of the graphics and design programs. Without your skills on vectorizing my images, my vision would not have come to life.

John Crusing:

My awesome cousin who believed in my ability and helped me reach my goal. Without your generosity my goal of completing my vision would have been much harder. Thank you for sending me an iPad for the purpose of seeing my vision and illustrations come to life.

Cindy Crusing:

Thank you for contributing to the completion of my vision. Thank you for giving me a stylus pen to use for my illustrations. You have always believed in me and I have found memories of us crafting at Grandma Crowe's house.

FINDING SUSAN

I got a dark sense of humor and a really quick temper
I got a husband who said "I really want to kiss her"

I got therapy twice a month and short sense of bliss
I got thoughts in my brain and I'm super sick of this

Cut my hair in a mohawk and painted my nails
Someone ought to stop me, I'm coming off the rails

Got a camera in my hand and a ranger in my pocket
Got a picture of my siblings hanging in my locket

The lyrics in my head, they never seem to stop
Listen to all music from bluegrass to pop

I got dreams so big they might just explode
I got issues everyday, I'm trying to unload

I would quit my day job if I could afford
I've got plenty to do and I'd never get bored

Out here in this life, in my head all the time
Finding a reason, a rhythm and a rhyme

WHAT CAN'T BE UNDONE

Her face was red from the rage she felt
The tears dried fast as her heart melts
The lies she found to be only truth
She stood on the edge of the unhinged roof
Her voice shook as she screamed
Nothing was at all as it seemed
Life was a lie and fiction was life
In her right hand she gripped the knife
To her throat she drew close the blade
In her mind the decision was made
Time was harsh and the season drew cold
This planet was boring and her thoughts old
Her face lifted up to the dark night sky
She yelled out the question "WHO AM I ?"
Tears falling down like rain on the ocean
She could end it all with one quick motion
But out of the dark came a voice from afar
Telling her to stop and count every star
Grasp hold of time and make it your own
Vibrations from the universe in a soft smooth tone
Stepping back from the edge of the roof
Still holding the knife asking for truth
She fell to her knees and looked to the ground
Still alone she made her way down
The voice clashes with those in her brain
Time is a question that continues to strain
But for now in this moment she hears only one
It kept her from doing what can't be undone

I WANT TO LIVE

The sky was painted pink and blue
We laid underneath the sunset
The water crashed upon the banks
Fireflies lit up with a yellow hue

Flower petals floated to the ground
I stumbled over my words
In the distance a melodic song
It was the most beautiful sound

Take my hand let's go astray
Don't leave me this way
Come on let's run away

Today I felt a smile across my face
The sky opened and hugged me
Cried once again but laughed out loud
Floating through time and space

In the distance I want to live
The grass under my feet is dying
I run to the edge of life
I still have so much to give

Take my hand let's go astray
Don't leave me this way
Come on let's run away

<u>REGRETS</u>

He felt her hand touch his face
One single tear shed from his eye
She kissed his forehead one last time
He whispered her name with a sigh
Slumped down in front of the stone
Opened his eyes he was alone
He missed her so much it hurt
Wishing it was him under the dirt
One month ago he declared his love
Took her hand in his and placed a ring
Devoted he was and wanted to show
But fate tore apart their dream
Whirlwind and fire set ablaze
Wishing he could take back those days
She was his sun and his moon
At night they named the constellations
He found his home in her heart
Life was to be their own creations
But now slumped in front of the stone
Opened his eyes he was alone
He missed her so much it hurt
Wished it was him under the dirt
Wished for his angel in his arms
Wishing he could have saved her from harm

FOREVER LOVE

It was a hot summer night
No stars in sight
The sun shared its light
The planets lined up right

Held hands like teenagers
Made plans like free rangers
Party like it's a rager
Sing love songs in key major

It was a cold winter morning
Life was far from boring
Poked your side cause of snoring
Looked in your eyes so adoring

Lips met like in tales of romance
Held me tight while we dance
Fell in love at first glance
Jumped straight in, took a chance

Fall then once came around
Leaves lay dying on the ground
My ears do love your voice sound
Time is motionless then it bounds

Your touch brings geese upon my skin
The warmth does rise from within
The world spins round once again
Hold me close it's time to begin

Spring jumps forth bright one day
Flowers of color flow and sway
Hear the music lovely play
Hearts melt together to stay

The planets form the universe
Only better never worse
Life can never be rehearsed
My love for you forever bursts.

ENTER PLAYER 2

Enter player 2
Press select and let's go
As Luigi is to Mario
You add extra hearts to my life
As Doug pines for Patty to be his wife
As Helga constructs a shrine
Forever, you will be mine
Plot twist
Like when Lois and Superman kiss
When the tide turned and ghosts turn blue
Enter player 2
Just as amazing as Link fishing in 64
You make my heart beat more
Green and Pink morph together
Just like when Monica found Chandler
Rocko to Spunky
SpongeBob to Gary
The writing on the dumpster
Forever he "dolphin chirp" loves her
When the flag raises
And the firework blazes
My love for you
Forever flames true
My eternal player 2

MAYBE ONE DAY

Go ahead pull the trigger no one will miss ya
Last chance to drink away the pain and kiss ya

Drowning the words that mess me up
Looking in the mirror to dress it up

Bang bang no one can hear the your body thump
Three days later drunk in a corner, body slump

Time is blurred, clock arms handless
Time is becoming pointless

Fighting the dark inside my head
Voices telling me I'd be better off dead

Tell me you love me
Tell me you'd miss me

Scream louder this time and in my face
Promise me you're not mad and I'm not a disgrace

Love me louder than I hate myself
Heal me deeper than I hurt myself

Wishing I was not this way
Maybe one day, Maybe one day

STAY

Hey you with the white shirt on
I see you all alone
Tell me your pain and I will tell you mine
I'm alone too all the time
I hear your pain and see
You feel just like me
Put down the gun it's ok
Please know you want to stay
So many people love you
So many things to do

Hey you with the white shirt on
I hear your hurt in your song
I know that pain and tears
Cuts to the bone all these years
Put down the gun it's ok
Please know you want to stay
So many people love you
So many things to do

Hey you with the white shirt red
Know it's all in your head
Hold on I'm here with you
Know I'm alone too
Life kicks while your down
Right now, stay safe and sound
Put down the gun it's ok
Please know you want to stay
So many people love you
So many things to do

TRUE LOVE

Julie went to school in the 80's
She loved Frank to death
She wanted his name and babies
He wanted head and beer breath

Friday nights she marched in the band
Frank smoked behind the bleachers
Held his keys and cigarette in his hand
Got impatient waiting to meet her

Julie wore pink lipstick, her hair in bows
Frank had holes in his jeans
When she graduated he was front row
They were just love struck teens

Frank worked as a mechanic
Julie sang their song
People said they wouldn't make it
But they proved them wrong

LAST PEAR

You were there
When I was in despair
I scratched your back
You washed my hair
But instead of shampoo you used Nair
My head was naked and felt so bare
I scratched so hard I heard your shirt tear
Oops, now we're even
You with no shirt and me with no hair
And the funny thing is we just don't care
This all started when I was in despair
Because the stupid goat ate the last pear.

PINK FLAMINGO

Have you ever had someone stare at you?
With their eyes fixed like glue?
I did once, by a pink flamingo names Blue
He sat and stared without a clue
That I was staring too.
Now this might be new to you
That a pink flamingo named Blue
Could be on this earth with nothing to do
But sit and stare at not me but you
It's amazing huh? That it could be true
That a pink flamingo named Blue
Could be staring at me, but looking at you

11

MY WAY

Don't tell me what to do
'Cause I'll walk the other way
You want me to conform
But I have my own brain
Tell me one more time
How my image defines
But don't expect me to abide
and I'll step out of line
You think I care for your thoughts
about what I do
But truth be told
I have no thoughts about you
You make me sick
with all your demands
Get out of my face and
untie my broken hands
Society says a woman
must be skinny with long hair
I break the rules and shave
both sides of my head bare
Paint your face and strut this way
in heels and low-cut skirts
Never mind your dress code
I wears guys pants and shirts
Let me live free from
your lies of who I am
Let me choose my path to walk
'cause I'm a wolf not a lamb

HER NAME

She walked down the street, her hands in her pockets
Looking for her car and the key to unlock it
Out of the darkness came a wind
That brought something dreary back again
Her hair moved slowly around her face
She moved faster with no time to waste
Reaching the door, she put in the key
Turned it to the right, sadly didn't see

A few days later while out in a crowd
She heard her name shouted out loud
Looking around she could not tell
If anyone at all had made that yell
The air became thick and wet like rain
Visions of death, suffering and pain
Her knees buckled as she spun around
The screams she made startled the crowd

Days later as she awakened the same
A voice once more whispered her name
What seemed like a moment was stillness in time
Entering the darkness, no light to shine
Back on the street she walked once more
In her mind the visions from before

Wind howling and screaming her name
A familiar character but never the same
This time no hiding or away swiftly running
She wanted to see who was so maliciously cunning
As the figure drew closer her breath turned to dust
He was tall and thin, with skin like rust
Reaching his hand close to her face
He disappeared without a trace

As she lay on her deathbed, cradling her sanity
The car keys lay on her antique vanity
Out of the silence once more is heard
A familiar voice saying that word
Her name was said once, twice and more
As the rust like hand opened the door

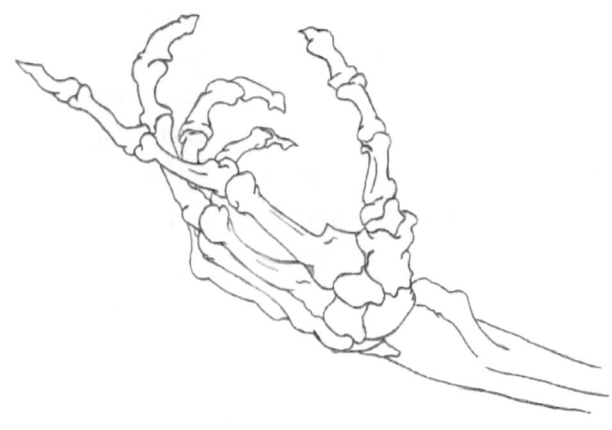

SOMETIMES

Sometimes is a relevant word
Yet, relevance can be absurd
When the eyes are cold and blackness looms
Only to find fear in our doom
Talking loudly to an empty space
To be staring at one's only face
And to think of what might have been
From now until then
Sometimes a word used with confidence
Yet, extinguishes the cost of it
And the hands have no touch to lift
And the feet are not swift
So, into the abyss the body tumbles
To awake to loudness and rumbles
Sometimes it is easy to let go
Yet, harder to find the flow
While the bodies electrical unit sleeps
The emotions weep
The darkness becomes reality
No time for afternoon tea
And time becomes nothingness
Into the soul it shall regress
Sometimes...

THE VEIL

Then there's the moment
The time when you lose it

The days when I'm in my head
The days when I wish I was dead

They come and go more often than not
They let me know, control I have not

Then it's dark and light chases
The time stands still yet races

The days are here and gone once more
The days I wonder what it's all for

Life is short before it's begun
And thinking in circles gets the job done

There's a moment in time
When all seems fine

And then the veil falls around
And my knees hit the ground

WAS IT A DREAM

Half past midnight she opened the door
The sun showered the flowers like never before

The clouds were puffy and full of shapes
The dog was barking over by the gate

She walked down the stairs and through the yard
Because of the dog she was on her guard

Reaching out to unlock the latch
The dog lunged hoping to catch

A little green being about 3 feet tall
The little being jumped back only to fall

With outstretched limbs his mouth opened wide
What a crazy day in the countryside

She grabbed the dog's collar and pulled him back
The little green being was under attack

He sprung to his feet and pulled out a taser
It looked like a toy so this did not phase her

She asked what he was and what he wanted
He looked at her as his eyes haunted

Chills ran down and up her spine
She reassured herself everything was fine

She looked him over again and again
Thinking an adventure was about to begin

The little green being held out his hand
A ship appeared but did not land

She sat up quickly in her bed
Could that have been all in her head

Walking in the kitchen she let out a sigh
His taser once more caught her eye

As she turned on the light
Again, she was filled with wonder and fright

NOW AND FOREVER

You are my rising sun and setting moon
I hope to love you soon

Far away from me you ran
Not knowing I'm your biggest fan

I watch you from afar
Wanting to be where you are

I scream out your name
Praying you're doing the same

Not knowing you in my mind
Is something I strive to find

Loving you more and more
You are the one I adore

You are my soul and my heart
With you I want my life to start

So, stand with me
At the bottom of the sea

And we will be together
Now and forever

WISHING

It's four in the morning and I'm still here
Sittin' on the bar stool sippin' on this beer

Talkin' to myself way too loud
Tryin' to talk over the imaginary crowd

Lost in my world of uncertainties
Tryin' not to become one of the casualties

Looking for the reason I'm here alone
Wondering why I can't find home

One match left unburned
One rock left unturned

With a dollar in my pocket
And your picture in my locket

I will sit at the bar
Wishing upon my star.

DREAM

I lay in the grass
And look at the stars
The sky is so clear
I think I see Mars
The sky is so simple
So complex and so deep
Why can't I see this,
when I'm not asleep
I open my eyes
And slowly discover
I'm not in the grass
But under the cover
The room starts to spin
I'm floating in space
And I feel once again
What a freakin' nut case
So now I'm on Mars
By myself
Watching the stars
I think I'll stay
On this planet
Out of the way
Only for awhile
'till I come back
with a smile

?

Love, time, space, fear
    What the hell am I doing here?
Hands, feet, lips, eyes
    Will the answer be a surprise?
Toes, fingers, spleen, heart
    It's all unclear when we're apart
Moon, stars, sun, sky
    It's so confusing I'm about to cry
Grass, birds, flowers, trees
    Tell me can you answer please?
What does this all mean?
    Who knows? Who cares?
We all end up somewhere…

DIRT

Death knocks upon my door
But I'm too busy rolling on the floor
Time flies by so fast
Why, just this morning is the past
I talk so loudly that no one hears
My millions and millions of fears
I care for no one but me
So, I run out towards the sea
My soul is dead
Or did I just go to bed
Without you I just hurt
But what can I do? You're under the dirt

22

TIRED

I can't keep up this masquerade
My mind is starting to fade

Life is such a game
That all the pieces look the same

One wrong turn with precision
Put you in the ground no decision

Strap up those boots it's getting thick
Run only to stop quick

Yeah, here we go up and down
Yet, at the end they steal your crown

Up the street people call my name
Wanting me to do the same

Just want to close my eyes
So go ahead and say those goodbyes

THE RAINBOW

Dance like you are the rainbow in a colorblind world

Mr. Sandman has come and gone
Lullabies of the haunted one
Feet to the floor and on with the day
Fix your face the world doesn't sway
Judgment comes in all forms
Never give in, never conform
Beating hearts, the kick drum starts

Dance like you are the rainbow in a colorblind world

The music drowns sorrows and lies
It soothes the hurt and babies' cries
Walk tall, don't bend your head
They may scream but you're not dead
Find the strength and let it go
Your spirits bright so let it flow
Breaking through your tear-filled eyes
Breaking through the worlds lies
Your beauty shines on a rainy day
Never put that shine away

Dance like you are the rainbow in a colorblind world

RAMBLE

Don't stop
      Ball drop
  Up top
       Flip flop
Drivin' home
      All alone
Down to stone
      Garden gnome
  Little hat
      Tires flat
Knowing that
      Black cat
On the roof
      Bullet proof
Cloven hoof
      Fireproof
Strong enough
      In the buff
Sliding stuff
      Being rough
The boys play
      Out all day
Sifting hay
      Run away
Tell a friend
      Not to send
Around the bend
      The end

25

DEATH

The sky let out a hellacious moan
The road upcoming was unknown

He said to me, "come down off the ledge"
I raised my hand to the knifes edge

And the sky yelled out for me to stop
Yet, all I saw was a flash and a pop

The lights went dim that night so sad
Death really isn't all that bad

Yet, death did not come so bitter sweet
My end that night I did not meet

The sky chuckled as I fell from grace
That night on the street such a disgrace

Teardrops in the night does anyone care
Death looks at me with his cold dark stare

YO, BRO

When the music starts it's time to run
Up ahead is jump number one
Mushrooms with feet, plants trying to eat
Down into the sewer I go
It's a nice day for a stroll
Break some bricks and kills some turtles
On to the next level, no matter the hurdles
Oh, look a castle filled with the dead
Better duck the fire balls to keep my head
Deadly villains, mushrooms that talk
Clouds with coins up a bean stalk
Hold my breath for quite awhile
All these fish bring a smile
Oh, crap! They are trying to bite
Swim, swim, swim with all my might
Afraid of heights and falling down
Top of the stairs where the fireworks sound
Flying fish, bullets that smile
I've ran for hours under a mile
They journey is coming to a close
Until next time, Love you bro.

26 COPYCAT TRAIL

26 Copycat Trail
The monster within told a tale
Laugh out loud jokes
Dragons and ghosts
Up and down the halls he roams
Getting drunk in the catacombs
At 26 Copycat Trail
The monster within sits for a spell
Down to the lab in the dungeon so dark
Out of his chest beats his heart
Cobwebs abound
No stir or sound
The residence at 26 Copycat Trail
Once alive but dead with betrayal
Around the corner by candle light
Once built on love but now fright
The haunting sound of the silence within
The monster sits and tries to pretend
All is alive and well
Inside 26 Copycat Trail

A DAY IN THE LIFE OF A SLUG

Today I moved 2 inches
Someone almost stepped on me
That was a terrifying moment
What is that?
A giant beast is smelling me
My slime trail is slowly fading
I've been working on it for days
These little brown chucks taste great
But every time I crawl on one
the beast takes it away
I have to keep moving
If the beast doesn't kill me
I will move 2 more inches
Be careful of the white poison
You will surely shrivel and
die if contact is made
Oh, look another slime trail
Frank must have been here
Oh well,
maybe I will catch up with him in a week or so
But for now, I travel alone

MINI GOLF DAY

It's mini golf day
Yay!
Tee box ready
Hands steady
Putter to ball
Off the wall
In for an ace
Special place
It's mini golf day
Yay!

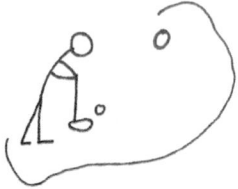

WHY I LIKE BEING A CAT

Free places to sleep
Lots of yummy treats
Big windows to look out of
Lots of things in high places to shove
Belly rubs

HANDS OF YOU AND I

Holding hands out in a field
The flowers wilt and die
But love flows through
The hands of you and I
So, the sun shines down
Out over the earth
And the time stands still
For what it's worth
The world doesn't care
If we should die
But time lives on
Through the hands of you and I
In the field once alone
Partners now, not on our own
Face the darkness
Let the sun shine
Our hands intertwined
Warm embraces from the sky
While love flows through
The hands of you and I

THE MAN IN THE RED COAT

I stood there listening to the wind through the trees
The man in the red coat appeared
The song of the willows brought me to my knees
He was everything I feared
Falling down the hill I cut my arms
He followed swiftly as I ran from him
I knew in my heart he meant me harm
The red coat started to unravel at the hem
Looking into his cold black eyes
He moved closer to my face
Over compensating for his size
I braced for his embrace
Howling at the pink full moon
In a moment the wolf pack appears
Standing at my side so soon
They attack him with my cheers
Red runs down the road
Blood soaked his coat
The one whose soul was sold
Sacrificed like a goat

ALONE

Falling to his knees hitting the ground with a thud
Slowly he grasped the loose dirt as hard as he could

Dirt fell through his fingers and the tears from his eyes
Beat his chest and thrust his face to the sky

Opening his mouth and out with a scream
Things were indeed as bad as they seemed

Falling face first to the ground he wept
Her secret forever he kept

As the wind began to blow
The sky grew angry, dark and low

The wind howled and the earth began to moan
As his heart broke, he was alone

ISSUES

I got issues
Most of them with you
I got fight
Most every night
I got anger
Never learned to tame her
I got loss
Emotions made of frost
I got pain
But not gain
I got time
Keep that in mind
I got issues
Most of them with you

SOCIAL MEDIA STALKER

Social media talking
Social media stalking
You watch me from afar
Never want to know who you are
Social media strutting
Social media fronting
Making it seem as if I like you
You don't know me true
Watching me live my best
Wanted credit for the rest
Social media talking
Social media stalking
Your face makes my eyes bleed
You're not what I need
Words about me but never to me
Want people to think you know me
Social media strutting
Social media fronting

DOWN BY THE RIVER

Down to the river I leisurely stroll
Walking along with my dog in tow
He loves the water on a hot day
He can be eccentric and spoiled that way
Looking out, skipping rocks
In my mind a memory knocks
A smile shines bright and my eyes look on
Even though you are gone
My dog runs wild and sees a bunny
"No! No!" I yell "he'll bite you honey"
But on they run and run and run
I can tell he's having fun
The sun starts to fade and night comes in
We will do this again and again
Traveling home, along with my
friend
We snuggle up on the couch
for the day to end

TURN AND RUN CUE

Told you once I was beginning to hate you
Should have taken that as my turn and run cue

Your words cut deep like a knife to the chest
Tried to leave because it was for the best

Always stayed because I thought you'd come around
I should have killed you when you were sleeping sound

Lying next to you thinking it was true
But the next day, found it was a nightmare times two

I told you once I was beginning to hate you
I should have taken that as my turn and run cue

You messed with my life, my mind and my reality
Kissed me, killed me and left me for eternity

I'm smarter than this yet I let you destroy
Thought I was better but turned out to be your toy

I hate you forever and yet you haunt my dreams
I'll never defeat your destruction it seems

I told you once I was beginning to hate you
I should have taken that as my turn and run cue

EULOGY

I remember you not so fondly
In my brain memories haunt me
The time you promised
And never came through
The times you said you would
But never did do
Words mean nothing because of you
Now your gone and we are gathered here
To lay you to rest and hold you dear
But I'm pretty sure hate fills this room
No tears to wipe away
People leaving soon
I'll watch them lower you into the ground
Make sure it's done
Make sure your 6 feet down
No longer can you say your lies
Just a day of last goodbyes
So go on down where I know you are
Leave me hear with one big scar
Time heals wounds I've heard them say
Hopefully I'll heal one day
Your death brings closure to a life of hurt
I do not cry as they cover you with dirt

SEARCHING

In my mind I stumble around
I wipe my face and push the ground
Away.
From my feet and into my hands
My memories have formed bands
That bind.
The water crashes and the sky fills
All around the wind kills
Dreams.
Formed from the start and out in space
Thoughts of laughter I have chased
Away.
The dark places of my mind have light
Out in front in clear daylight
Blindness.
How can it be so blindly clear?
That no one can ever escape the fear
Failure.
My mind is a web of deceptions and truth
I stand on the highest mountain with proof
Why?
Questions of new and old appear
The time has come it is too cold here
Time.
So onward I stumble with flashlight in hand
To find the one who can release the band
Freedom.

<u>GIRL</u>

I'm in my t-shirt and pearls
Hawk all in curls

Definition of a girl

My face in lights
Tell me all the time
Step in line
Slim that behind

To be a definition of a girl

Music up loud
Standing in the crowd
Singing lyrics loud
Dancing big and proud

Representing all girls

<u>BOAT</u>

Sailed a boat to the horizon
Fell off into the deep
At first your lies were mesmerizing
But promises you just wouldn't keep

You slipped out from my hands
Right into my nightmares
Crashed the boat into the sands
On the island of no one cares

Sailing by the stars in the night sky
Distance was an inevitable curse
For love between you and I
Would make things much worse

The horizon slipping away
The sunset is fading fast
Drowning slower day by day
The boat has sunk at last

No more hurting from
the splintered planks
No more pain to come
On the safe banks

JUST BE YOU

So much pressure to be perfect
Get it together to be worth it

But I got news for all who doubt
Perfect is not what I'm about

Life is messy and not refined
Keep that close and in mind

It's ok to try something new
It's ok to find it's not for you

Judgments will come left and right
Just try your best both day and night

Cut your hair or grow it long
Learn a new hobby or write a song

Keep on embracing things new to you
Being yourself in all that you do

TOMMY

Tommy sat at the bar with a whiskey in his hand
Thinking of her while listening to the band
His head running in circles as his brain can't understand
Bartender asked, "Will that be all, man?"
Tommy left the bar headed for her home
Knew when he got there, she wouldn't be alone
Walked through the grass past his car with all the chrome
Smashed in his windshield with a broken garden gnome
Blue lights and sirens filled the night air
Tommy knew who exactly would be there
Blood ran bright down the front of the stair
Soaked through her shirt and long blonde hair
Tommy laid beside her with his chest opened wide
The killer on the run with no place to hide
All three knew the truth but only two lied
Tommy could have lived, but never left her side

Janie opened the door for Jack to enter
He had flowers and leaned down to kiss her
They met at Tommy's 4 month ago last winter
She thought he was rugged and her tinder
On the couch his hand on her knee
Her hair smelt of coconut and green tea
Embracing each other all through the movie
One they would have to watch again to really see
Caught up in the moment lost in each other
A crash from outside startled the lovers
Out in the yard it was Tommy, no other

To tell Janie he was the one who loved her
Bright red blood stained the officer's shirt
He leaned down as he touched the dirt
Tommy and Janie were more than hurt
The neighbor was the police alert

Jack jumped to his feet as he heard the crash
He and Tommy were about to clash
As he opened up the door, he saw the flash
As he fell to the floor, he saw his past
Janie let out a long high scream
Nothing was about to be as it seemed
Jack laid dying like a movie scene
Tommy motionless couldn't believe what he'd seen
The killer turned towards Tommy standing in the yard
Janie ran to hit him but not that hard
Another shot rang out with her chest being marred
Tommy was too late to be her bodyguard
As she fell to the porch blood gushing out
Tommy cried tears and let out a shout
The killer took one more pull as the gun rang out
Tommy held Janie's hand as the blood poured about

THE BRIDGE

The night was darker than normal
They stood on the bridge in the rain
He climbed on the wrong side of the rail
And put the gun to his brain
Tears streaming down her face
She begged him to come home
The pain was more than he could bare
She promised he wasn't alone
The night air was cold and wet
The full moon was hidden by the clouds
These are the words she said to him
As she screamed them out loud
"Please come down off the ledge
Please come home I love you
Please don't do this to yourself
If you die then I die too
Please let me inside
I want to hold you and kiss your face
It's ok to be sad and mad
It ok for your pain to embrace
I'm in this with you my love

Just come home with me
Take the gun from your head
And let the sadness be
We can fix anything that is broken
We can love anything that is sad
We can get through it all together
But if you die that's bad
Please my love hear me
Feel my words in your heart
Where you are right now
Will tear us both apart"
His hand shook with exhaustion
As her words touched his brain
He knew he wanted to end it all
But it was really just the pain
He closed his eyes and let out a scream
Looked her in the eyes
And threw the gun in the stream
Back on the bridge together
She wiped away his tears
He never fully recovered
But they loved all through the years

HIT WITH REALITY

I feel stupid and annoying
Like my life has become boring
You think you know all there is
Like your life is above this
Act all high and mighty towards me
But come on down and you will see
I was then and am now
Going to be ok somehow
Thought better of what you are
Thought you would follow me far
But in the end, you are just the same
So tired of playing y'all's silly game
I feel tired and useless
Like my life is a sickness
Sorry for interrupting your superiority
I tend to forget I'm no priority

I was right from the beginning
Thought your love I was winning
But you didn't want me then
Why did you even try to pretend
From his shadow step outside
Your dislike needs to no longer hide
Killed my spirit and my love
Feelings died for all above
I should have believed my thoughts in the past
They told me I meant nothing and you wouldn't last
Thinking you cared when you really just pretend
Today I believe my past self in the end
I won't call or write and bother you at all
Today is the last when you made my heart fall

<u>THEY</u>

She had a lifetime of scars
She tried to drown in the bars
Her time was running short
And all she did was snort
He had a pocket that was empty
He was the ripe old age of 20
His time was running short
And all he did was snort

They met on the street
No shoes on their feet
Their addiction trying to beat

She had dirty blonde hair
That stretched down to there
Her time was almost done
And all she did was run
He had a white tattered shirt
Covered in brown dirt
His time was almost done
And all he could do was run

Their fate they met that night
On the bridge under the moonlight
Death found them holding on tight

BURY THE PAST

A broken car on the side of the road
A story of love left untold
Running in circles to find the exit
Only to know right where you left it
Drunk again on whiskey and pain
Nothing to know and nothing to gain
Let the past stay buried and follow the stream
Move forward from this bad dream
The words were written and lost in the dark
No light to know, no path to embark
You are thriving and loving life
No need to re-stir all that strife
He used her, yes, that is true
But there is nothing for you to do
History cannot hurt if you face it on
Let dead dogs lie and be gone
Broken heart blood pouring out
No one knows what it's all about
Without the chaos and deception
Life would not have known your conception
From the dark and painful lies
Emerged a girl with star-gazing eyes
To see the world and wonders of great
To love yourself it's not too late

MUSIC FROM WITHIN

I feel the drum beat in my chest
The lyrics talk
My mind does the rest

I see the pictures in my eyes
I hear the pain
Of the goodbyes

Looking for love in the dark
Finding what's left
Our story arc

Falling sideways down the stairs
It was the night
I held your hair

The music kicked in once again
We laughed until
Our stomach gave in

Now all I have is a polaroid
Of us on the floor
Inside the pizza joint

Nothing consoles my emptiness
Not the music
Or the friendliness

People are shells of you
Their souls tell a tale
And out of the blue

Your visions appear next to me
Your smell haunts
For eternity

What was once a fairytale
Is now a plot
Straight from hell

The music once more in my chest
The lyrics lie
Just like the rest

THESE THOUGHTS

These thoughts are eating me alive
These pills are killing me from inside
I look for the light in my eyes
Said my goodbyes

This time it's different inside my head
Felt a bit better but then felt dead
Putting my feelings behind what's said
Untouched cures under the bed

These thoughts are tearing up my heart
These pills were a mistake from the start
My face tells the story falling apart
Put the rest in the cart

Pull the lever let it fly
Goodbye
So, this is the end of you and I
Dead inside

Yet here we are with this again
Can I call you friend
Do you care if I blend in
Do you care if I end

These thoughts are eating me alive
These pills are killing me from inside
I look for the light in my eyes
Said my goodbyes

Shouting out for your hand
Let's take time in the land
Let's make love once again
Fall to pieces in the end

RUNNING SCARED

Running scared in the dark
She stopped at the park

Looked side to side and forward to back
Heart pounding like an attack

Looking at the light from the moon
Knowing he would be there soon

Wanting to exhale into the air
Holding her breath while standing there

One more step towards the pale tree
One more step to let it be

Was she alone on the street that night
Was she wrong or was she right

The thoughts in her head played tricks
The clock on her wrist made ticks

Hour by hour, minute by minute
The seconds were the hardest when in it

Up with the sun
No place to run

She sat waiting for the bus
No one to listen to her fuss

He left years or decades ago
Time moves extra slow

Haunted by what used to be
Never out running eternity

Running scared in the dark
She stopped at the park

Where they had their last kiss
The one she will always miss

ANXIOUS MEMORY

I'm sipping on a cocktail of anxiety and a memory
All this thinking is killing me

Do you ever get tired for no reason
No matter the time or the season

Sliding across the universe
All forward no reverse

Little green men stop to talk
While out on my space walk

Out of my head and down inside
When worlds collide

Need to feel alive and heard
Spoken is the silent word

Looking in the mirror all I see
Is this cocktail of anxiety and a memory

<u>FATE</u>

And when the darkness sets in the fading sun
The time will reverse and the show has begun

Deep within my gaping chest a heart beats cold
In the field so doomed to die runs the stream of old

And in the brightness once dim with strife
Shines a light so full with life

The planets set unto their course
And once again with magnetic force

The darkness dooms upon my face
I'm damned to die within this place

FIGHTING HISTORY

Shattered glass upon the floor
Beautiful vase you are no more

They broke your soul and killed your spirit
Almost succeeded in taking you with it

History once repeated
The show is started, please be seated

Your innocence lost so young of age
The story is the same on every page

Searching for something you are without
When within yourself you twist and doubt

Knowing how but never when
Knowing nothing all over again

They cut you off at the knees
Made you cry, beg and plead

Inside your brain they cut the wires
Made you believe they were not liars

All this time you've broken down
Stayed trapped inside this broken town

They built the walls and sealed the door
In this house you stay no more

Take the hammer in your hand
Break open your life and break the band

Once in your head and on the floor
Broken glass you are no more

Kill their words and spirit too
They cannot tell you what to do

Feel the pain and set it free
Be the woman you are meant to be

I WILL SHELTER YOU

When the tears fall like rain
And the questions bring pain

When you just can't weather the storm
And your too far from shore

Reach out to me and I'll shelter you
Until black skies turn to blue

Until the rains wash away
I'll keep the storms far away

When you just can't take anymore
And life is banging down your door

When all you can do is open your eyes
I see and hear your cries

Reach out to me and I'll shelter you
Until black skies turn to blue

Until the rains wash away
I'll keep the storms far away

When the past come rolling in
And all you know is deep within

When blinding lights turn to dark
And anger ignites with a spark

Reach out to me and I'll shelter you
Until black skies turn to blue

Until the rains wash away
I'll keep the storms far away

I'll keep you safe and sound
Your secrets whistling 'round

Take my hand I'll lead you home
To a place that's safe to roam

IT'S BEEN A LONG DAY

It's 3 am and I begin
Up to work and down the bend

People in and people out
Crying, cursing, loving shout

Heavy times and heavy things
People with their trouble sings

It's been a long day
I'm sick to the bone
Show me the way
To get back home

6 pm dead again
Sun still up with a twin

Brightness blinds
And time intertwines

The cries from my thoughts
All must be lost

It's been a long day
I'm sick to the bone
Show me the way
To get back home

NO NEED

You took my secrets and used them against me
You let the wall fall on me

You pushed me to my limit
You took my light and tried to dim it

So, I cut you off and said goodbye
No need to hurt or to cry

Every picture cut out your face
We were over at a rapid pace

You took my love and deceived me
You gave them the key

To the car to run me down
Tied me and left me bound

Turned against me over night
Nothing about you is right

You pushed me to my limit
You took my light and tried to dim it

So, I cut you off and said goodbye
No need to hurt or to cry

ALL ALONE

No one around
No stars in the sky
No thoughts in my mind
No need to cry

The universe is filled
With people all around
But I'm alone
Lying on the ground

Dying flowers
Line my casket
No eyes to see
Or fill the basket

All alone in the crowd
All alone in my head
Sometimes life
Is full of dread

ABDUCTION

Looking at the moon
Astronaut in disguise
Men in black
Aliens hate those guys

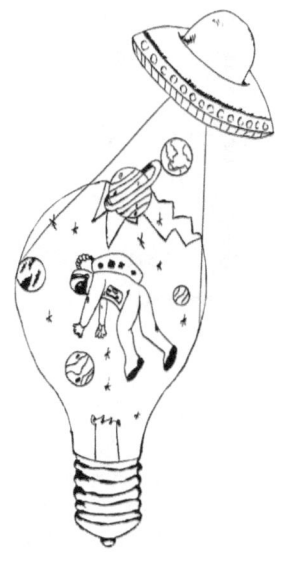

Cows in a field
Midnight in August
Green ray of light
Jealous to be honest

Take me with you
She yelled running wild
Earth was her home
Curious as a child

The cow mooed
Strobing lights spinning
round
News reports of a UFO
Lights burned the ground

Out in space with the moon
The sun shines bright
The cow would live
That August night

LIVING ON A LYRIC

Standing out in the rain with my bonnet
You took my heart and wrote your name upon it

You're the only bee for me
Sit down and share some tea

Cause I'll be there when you wake
No need for wet cheeks or a heart break

Let's take a long drive in the car
I don't care where or how far

Forever be my music man
Living life the best we can

You're the dream I was running too
I'll forever be your Suzie-Q

TAKE AND BREAK

I took a hit today
Lost another one along the way

Finding who my people are
The ones who love and do not scar

Take what's yours and leave the rest
Make life better, do your best

Stop hurting me and get off my throat
Stop being the hole in the sinking boat

Trusting people gets you hurt
Might as well be under the dirt

The ones who lied and loved no more
The ones who hit just to keep score

Trust was cut one more time
For every nickel they'll take a dime

Take, take, take
Is all they do

Break, break, break
The rest of you

BLACK SHEEP

Always the outsider from day one
Alone since my life begun
People telling me how to act
Like my own life was not fact
Black sheep in the family today
Black sheep from beyond yesterday
Never fit in and never belong
Same ol' dance, same ol' song
You look at me left to right
To get here I've had to fight
All alone in this world was I
All since the day when I began to cry
Victims to the left, victims to the right
I refuse to be one with all my might
What I am is what is me
Don't like what you see?
Then shut your eyes and turn your head
Pretend I'm already dead
I refuse to play by your rules
I will build my life using my tools
No need to tell me how you feel
To me you are far from real
I've made it this far without your approval
I'll make it farther after your removal

WHEN

When your lost in a moment
And can't control it
When the time stops cold
And your life feels old
When that friend has forsaken
And your heart is breakin'
When love fades away
And grows again another day
When the land beneath your feet
And the coffin does meet
When your life makes you cry
And the ash falls from the sky
When you finally learn to love
And yourself is who you love
When your questions turn to answers
And the fallen turn to dancers
When you join at the end of days
And the music just forever plays
When you know who you are
And you forever wish upon that star

DISAPPOINTMENT

I will forever be a disappointment, but I'm ok with that
Circling back to the start, replay the act

Don't want to forget and move past
Don't want to act bigger than the cast

They are the reason I act this way
From today and tomorrow to yesterday

Say how I feel and get torn apart
Looking to the end and a place to start

Move forward just to feel
Tell me my emotions are not real

Look me in the eye and in my face
Tell me how to win this race

Lie one more time to the world out there
Let me see me and begin to stare

If they judge I know the truth
Been this way since my youth

Disrespectful little brat
Let them continue to think that

I know the truth and what you've done
I know I'm not the only one

When the trauma hits and time won't heal
I will deal how I deal

Keep your thoughts and feelings to
Wrapped up inside you

That's what people always say
Well, I don't function that way

I hate and cry and laugh inside
You don't have to come for the ride

Stay in yours and I'll stay in mine
Without you I will shine

And when I burn brighter than the sun
You will know I have begun

And you are not welcome to come inside
Because to me you've already died

INVASION

Violence creeps around the sun
One by one the martians come
Did you lie upon the ground
Did you stand or fall down
I saw the sun dance with the moon
Words of old that made him swoon
The field of green embraced me tight
We fell in love once more that night
Lightning bugs among the heat
Flickered to our hearts beat
And in the distance little green men
Can't be more than 9 or 10
I raised my head to see how far
But was too late to throw a star
And in the moment the violence hit
And in the rubble we stop and sit
The sun went black upon the tide
The moon was sad and continuously cried
And in the darkness we heard a laugh
As the martians stole a calf
And in their ship they flew away
Maybe the sun will return one day

GIRL-HAWK

Small talk
Girl talk
Sailor talk
All with my Girl-hawk
Perspiration
Inspiration
Destination
Rockin' my Girl-hawk
Society breakin'
Barrier breakin'
No crap takin'
Girl with a Girl-hawk
Jewelry or no
Hair up let's go
Put on a show
With my Girl-hawk
Running that mile
Look up and smile
Inspire a child
All with my Girl-hawk
Finding myself
Take me up off that shelf
Loving myself
And my Girl-hawk
Nothing defines you
Like you do
Us girls will make it through
With our Girl-hawks

VIOLENCE IS NOT LOVE

He took his hand across her face
Invaded her mind and her space
He took her love and spent it all
Making her think she had to crawl
Love knows no violence in its core
Love is more than the time before
Love does not make you question life
Love is peaceful not filled with strife
He took her for granted one too many
She gave her all, she gave plenty
Once in a while he made her smile
But more times than most that's not his style
Love knows no violence in its core
Love is more than the time before
Love does not make you question life
Love is peaceful not filled with strife
He made life hard and simply unbearable
She stayed with him which was terrible
And who suffered most was the kids at home
Left to themselves in life to roam

MOVING FORWARD

In time wounds will heal and scars will form
Whoever is left after the storm
But I'll tell you this here and now
I will protect myself I vow
Boundaries will be set, the line in the sand drawn
When the smoke clears at the break of dawn
You will be gone from my sight
No more sad days, no more sleepless nights
Out in the cold you threw me long ago
Now it's my turn to rise from below
The thumb you tried to keep me under
Feel my rage, hear the thunder
Cause I'm awake with eyes wide open
Tired of the lies and words chokin'
Sick of you and all your manipulation
Time has given a chance for contemplation
So listen close as I sing my song
It won't say much and it won't take long
Some people will try to keep you down
They are the ones you don't want around
So if you can't raise my spirits
Shut your mouth cause I don't want to hear it

SAD SONGS

I hear a sad song and think about you
Tell me what else can I do
I've run in circles night and day
Trying to end the pain this way
Looking for you in the dark
I follow your path to embark
Upon a journey falling stars
Just to find where you are
Picking up a rock to throw
I'll only go where you go
Help me find you in this world
A story book boy and girl
Sadness rains in my mind
Light a match to only find
Darkness lingers both in the light
I'm too tired to win this fight
Sad songs and your memory beats
Winter fades and summer heats
I'll miss you later and after that
I miss our late-night chat
But sad songs will flow inside
From the day you left, I cried
Darkness takes control within
Sad songs play once again

CAN'T UNDO

Hold up that middle finger
Let that anger linger
Words rush like a raging river
Cutting you sliver by sliver
Drown those sorrows one by one
Can't erase what you've done
Broke my heart more than most
Made me long for a ghost
The thought of you resonates
But in a moment dissipates
Visions of violence returned in head
The part of you is now dead
I loved her once but you killed
That part of a child who was thrilled
To see your face through the glass
Now from you I just run fast
Anger and hate, rage on inside
Love for you forever died
And time moves forward away from you
What you've done you can't undo

THE LETTER

If I had to write you a letter
There would be 26 all together
You sucked the life right out of me
Made me older than I had to be
Wrote my future with your curse
Disregarded my whole worth
Took your position for your pleasure
Changed my position in forever
Far away I wish you'd stayed
My trust you utterly betrayed
Anger melts my thoughts within
I hate you now, I can't pretend
Death came and gave you grace
Yet to the world you are a disgrace
I was a kid with hopes and dreams
Torn from the pages, ripped at the seams
Thief of my time, my innocence
Never suffering the consequence
Lied to me from the start
Lied about me and my heart
Twisted my thoughts day and night
Begged me to stay inside the fight
Knowing your selfishness would harm
You carried on with no alarm
In the end I will hate you still
Your memory I'll try to kill
And as I walk away from you
All your destruction I'll try to undo

LIFE

Between existence and not
In this feeling I am caught

How do I put into words how I feel
Knowing the pain and joy are real

Time stands still and moves in reverse
Time speeds by unlike we'd rehearsed

Is this life or death in the making
I know your tired of my bellyaching

But I'm so lost in this mess of confusion
Waking up each day to a brand-new contusion

My brain is tired and sad at the same
Tired of playing this sick twisted game

Do I live or simply exist
Do I die in an unfortunate twist

The blood that flows through my veins
My thoughts that hurt and heal are the same

Please make it stop and I can rest
Instead of failing this never-ending test

FEAR

The clock struck midnight and all went dark
Only sound heard was a dog bark
Down the way a man clutched his chest
Her head made the decision and her hands the rest
The lights flickered as dusk moved towards dawn
Across town the show must go on

Men in top hats with mustaches
Find the roses among the ashes
Sitting up high looking down on the players
Their appearance is distinguished but their minds have
no layers
The curtain falls for one last night
Not knowing for their lives they'd have to fight

Thunder struck and silence broke
Heaviness set at midnight stroke
His hands cold with bones outstretched
Cover his head with his eyes convexed
Open his mouth without a sound
Only for his scream to push you down

Fear sets into the brain without knowing
Goosebumps appear as the fear is growing
Deep in the gut a turning and churning
The question of life inside is burning
Unsettled confounds inside your head
Is it alive or is it dead

SECRET

You want to tell me your secret
Don't worry I'll keep it
Wrap your arms tight
Hold out through the night
Don't let those voices
Determine your choices
Let the emotions flow
Let the sadness go
Look in my eyes see your face
Take your time feel the embrace
Don't give into what you see
Let your light shine take love from me
So, tell me your secret
I swear I'll keep it
No need to hide away
Let the smile return today
I'll take your burden
I know your hurtin'
Don't close the curtain
Hold on its ok
The pain will stop one day
Find the strength deep down
I'll make you smile from that frown
Please don't go just stay
I'll stay with you forever and a day

I SURVIVED YOU

I don't wish pain on you
That's not something I would do

But here's what I will say
You shouldn't have treated me that way

Time has passed and with it me
Never what I want it to be

I'll walk away with my head held high
I saved myself and didn't die

But not for lack of your trying
You left me sinking and crying

Threw me to the wolves for their lunch
But on their bones instead I crunch

You thought of me as your cross to bare
You made life hard and unfair

MOURNING

There is hate in my heart
For the one from where I start

You made me watch as you killed her slowly
Took away my one and only

I remember her voice of the stories she read
Kissed me good night and put me to bed

The way she smelled and her hugs were home
But now she's dead and I'm all alone

You killed my mother one step at a time
Tried to kill me but i stepped out of line

Her body, her face, even her name
You and her are one in the same

Forgiveness is not an option at this place
For once put me first and give me space

Let me mourn my mother and say goodbye
All I'm left with are memories and these tears I cry

SKELETONS IN YOUR CLOSET

Do you feel dead inside or all alive
Burning questions in your eyes

But the skeletons in your closet
Are not sitting on it

They are telling your secrets
You should've known not to keep it

Gunpowder breath
Scared to death

Finding your way through the forest
Four verses then the chorus

Muddy waters flowing past
Blood spills from broken glass

Shadows scatter into the day
It should not have ended this way

LIVE

I see you there with the tears in your eyes
On your knees screaming goodbyes

But take the gun from your head
Your heart is beating you are not dead

I know the darkness and the pain
I know the daily pressure and the strain

Put down the blade and lift your head
Your heart is beating you're not dead

Please hear me as I lose my voice
Your death and life is your choice

Inside it feels like a thunderstorm
But here in reality it's safe and warm

Step away from the ledge is what I said
Your heart is beating you are not dead

THE WAR IN MY HEAD

I'm lost in the sounds of my thoughts everyday
I'm getting tired of living this way

I want to be free of the doubt and fear
I want to love and laugh year after year

I hear you whisper to just go on and die
These words you said made me cry

I want to live long and happy
Why do you yell these things at me?

Please quiet down I can't handle this abuse
Can y'all please just be quiet and call a truce?

In my head a war is raging
Telling me I'm useless but beautifully aging

Inside the hurricane destroys
Outside the weapon deploys

I need to rest and turn off the sounds
But in my head bad thoughts abound

RAINING SINCE NOVEMBER

It's been raining since November
and I'm stuck here in Tennessee
Dead possum on the road side
Song birds in the trees
I'm looking for a turn of the tide
'Cause it's been raining since November

I keep thinking, but can't remember
Past the lines of Tennessee
Moonshine in the still
Dying leaves on the trees
I've been searching for a thrill
'Cause it's been raining since November

The fire has burned to its last ember
Out here in Tennessee
Smoke on the mountain
It's getting really hard to see
The days I keep countin'
'Cause it's been raining since November

Dear Susan,

You can go rest now little girl
I promise to protect your world
Rest my dear I know you're tired
Always on guard and always wired
Let those tears dry and wipe your face
We are together in our safe space
Please little one relax and rest
Please know I'm doing my best
Your anger and temper are hard to take
Let's calm down and take a break
I know your hurt and confused
You were broken and abused
But I'm here now and no one can
Ever hurt you like that again
So rest my child and let's take a ride
I'll hold you close always inside
We'll have those adventures that you never had
I'll buy those items you wanted so bad
Your safe and sound forever now
I love you little Susan, so rest for now.

A Letter to Myself

Hey there I know your down
But people love when your around
It may not seem so all the time
Life keeps messing with your mind
But deep inside is light and joy
Like when a child gets new toy
Like when the sunset turns to pink
Life is better than you think
So read these words all around
When your brain beats you down
When the rain doesn't bring a rainbow
And things don't your way go
You are fun, loving and creative
You do not need to be validated
But I'll go ahead and say it anyway
I love you and want you to stay
So read these words I've put down for you
When your happy and especially when blue

Until Next Time...

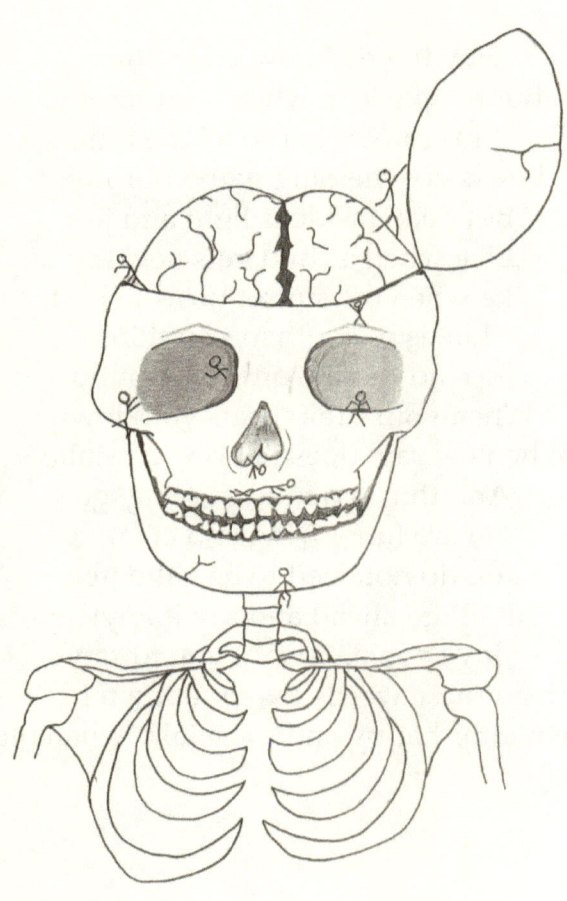

www.ingramcontent.com/pod-product-compliance
Lightning Source LLC
Chambersburg PA
CBHW021003150626
46549CB00012BA/1035